Noah Webster

Advice *to the* Young

&

Moral Catechism

Contents

[1] Excerpted from *History of the United States* by Noah Webster, LL.D.
published by Durrie & Peck (Concord 1832)
[2] Excerpted from *The American Spelling Book* (Boston 1798) pp. 145-52 -
[3] Excerpted from *The American Spelling Book* (Boston 1798) pp. 154-55 -

Advice *to the* Young

1. My young friends, the first years of your life are to be employed in learning those things which are to make you good citizens, useful members of society, and candidates for a happy state in another world. Among the first things you are to learn are your duties to your parents. These duties are commanded by God, and are necessary to your happiness in this life. The commands of God are, "Honor thy father and thy mother." - "Children, obey your parents in all things." These commands are binding on all children; they cannot be neglected without sin. Whatever God has commanded us to do, we must perform, without calling into question the propriety of the command.

2. But the reasonableness of this command to obey parents is clear and easily understood by children, even when quite young. Parents are the natural guardians of their children. It is their duty to feed, clothe, protect, and educate them; and for these purposes it is proper and necessary that parents should have authority to direct their actions. Parents therefore are bound by duty and by right to govern their children; but the exercise of this right is to be regulated by affection. Parents have implanted in them a tender love for their offspring, which induces them to exercise authority over them with kindness.

3. It is proper that parents should be entrusted with the instruction of children, because children have everything to

learn, and parents are older and have gained a knowledge of what their children want to know. Parents have learned what is right, and what is wrong; what is duty, and what is sin; what is useful and what is hurtful to children and to men. And as children pass the first years of their life with their parents, they may be continually learning from their parents what is necessary or useful in their concerns of life.

4. It is not only proper that children should obey their parents, but their obedience should be prompt and cheerful. A slow, reluctant obedience, and that which is accompanied with murmurings, is not acceptable to parents nor to God. A sense of duty should make a child free and ready to comply with a parent's command; and this will always be the case where the child entertains a due respect for his parents. Love and respect render obedience easy and cheerful, and a willing obedience increases the confidence of parents in their children, and strengthens their attachment to them. But a cold and unwilling obedience, with a murmuring disposition, alienates affection, and inclines the parent to rigor and severity in exercise of his authority.

5. Hence it is a primary duty of children, and as much their interest as it is their duty to "Honor their father and mother." This honor not only forbids the child to disobey his parents but it forbids all rudeness and ill manners towards them. Children should manifest their respect for their parents in all their actions. They should be modest and respectful in their company, never interrupting them in conversation, nor boldly contradicting them: they should address them as superiors,

and yield to their opinions and admonitions. This subordination of children to their parents is the foundation of peace in families; contributes to foster those kindly dispositions, both in parents and children, which are the sources of domestic happiness, and which extend their influence to all social relations in subsequent periods of life.

6. Among the first and most important truths which you are to learn, are those which relate to God and religion. As soon as your minds become capable of reasoning, or excited by curiosity to know the causes of things, you will naturally inquire who made the world, who made you, and why were you made? You will understand, by a moment's thought, that the things around you cannot have made themselves. You will be convinced that a stone or a mass of earth cannot have made itself, as it has no power in itself to act or move; it must then have had a creator, some being that had power to act or move, and to bring the stone into existence.

7. You observe that plants and trees grow, but they do not grow in winter, when it is cold; some degree of heat is necessary to their growth. You conclude then that wood and vegetable matter in itself has not the power of growth or increase. You see various animals, as dogs, and horses, but you know that they cannot create themselves; the first animal of every kind must then have had a creator, distinct from the animal itself. You see houses, and barns and ships, but you know that they did not make themselves; you know they are made by men. You know also that you did not create yourselves; you began

to exist at a time which you cannot remember, and in a manner of which you have no knowledge.

8. From such familiar observations and reflections, children may be convinced, with absolute certainty, that there must be a being who has been the creator of all things which they see. Now when you think that of all the substances about you, not one can have been its own creator, and when you see the vast multitude of things, their variety, their size, their curious forms and structures, you will at once conclude that the Being who could make such things must possess immense power, altogether superior to the power of any being that you see on the earth. You will then be led to inquire who is this Being, and where is he.

9. Here not only children, but the wisest philosophers are brought to a stand. We are compelled to believe that there is a Being of vast and unlimited power, who has created whatever we see; but who he is or where he is, we cannot know by our own observation or reason. As we cannot see this Being, we cannot, by the help of reason, know anything of his manner of existence, or of his power, except what we learn from his works, or from revelation. If we had been left to gather all of our knowledge of the creator from his works, our knowledge of him must have been very imperfect. But the creator has not left mankind in ignorance on this subject. He has graciously revealed his character to man; and his revelations are recorded in a book, which by way of eminence, is called the *Bible*.

10. From the Bible we learn that God is a *Spirit*; hence we cannot see him. Spirit is not visible to human eyes. Yet we

8

need not wonder that a substance which is invisible should possess amazing power. We cannot see the air or wind; yet we know by observation, that this fine, subtle fluid is a substance that supports our life, and when in rapid motion, it has immense force. We conclude then that a Being, consisting of pure heart, may possess all the power necessary to the formation of the sun, moon, and stars, and everything that we can see or feel. This great Being, in our language, is called *God*. He is a spirit that extends through the universe.

11. The scriptures inform us that God is not only all-powerful, but all-wise: and his wisdom is played in admirable structure of whatever he has made; in the adaptation of everything to its proper uses; in the exact order and beautiful arrangement and harmony of all parts of creation.

The scriptures inform us also that God is a benevolent Being. "God is love," and we have abundant evidence of this truth in the works of creation. God has not only made man and animals, but he has furnished the earth with everything that is necessary for their support and welfare. The earth is stocked with plants, which are food for the animals, of various kinds, as well as for man; and plants and animals furnish man with food and clothing and shelter from the inclemency of the weather. The sea and the rivers and lakes are also stocked with animals that supply food and other conveniences for man. The earth contains inexhaustible stores for supplying the wants and desires of living creatures.

12. We learn also from the Bible that God is a holy Being; that is, he is perfectly free from any sinful attributes or

dispositions. If God was a wicked or malevolent Being, he would have contrived and formed everything on earth to make his creatures miserable. Instead of this, we know from observation as well as experience, he has made everything for their comfort and happiness. Having learned from the scriptures and from the works of creation, the character of God, and that he is your creator; the next inquiry is, in what relation do you stand to your maker, and what is his will respecting your conduct.

13. The first and most important point to be decided in your minds is that God is your *Supreme* or *Sovereign Ruler*. On this point, there can be no room for doubt; for nothing can be more evident than that the Being who creates another, has a perfect, indisputable right to govern him. God has then a complete right to direct all the actions of the beings he has made. To the lower animals God has given certain propensities, called instincts, which lead them to the means of their own subsistence and safety.

14. Man is a being of a higher order; he is furnished with understanding or intellect, and with powers of reason, by which he is able to understand what God requires of him, and to judge of what is right and wrong. These faculties are the attributes of the soul, or spiritual part of man, which constitutes him a moral being, and exalts him to a rank in creation much superior to that of any other creature on earth.

15. Being satisfied that God is your creator and rightful governor, the next inquiry is, what is his will concerning you; for what purpose did he make you and endow you with reason?

A wise being would not have made you without a wise purpose. It is very certain that God requires you to perform some duties, and fill some useful station among other beings.

16. The next inquiry then is, what you are to do and what you are to forbear, in order to act the part which your maker has assigned to you in the world. This you cannot know with certainty without the help of revelation. But here you are not left without the means of knowledge; for God has revealed his will, and has given commands for the regulation of your conduct.

17. The Bible contains the commands of God; that book is full of rules to direct your conduct on earth; and from that book you may obtain all you want to know, respecting your relation to God, and to your fellow men, and respecting the duties which these relations require you to perform. Your duties are comprised in two classes; one including such as are to be performed directly to God himself; the other, those which are to be performed directly to your fellow men.

18. The first and great command is, to love the Lord your God with all the heart and soul and mind and strength. This supreme love to God is the first, the great, the indispensable duty of every rational being. Without this no person can yield acceptable obedience to his maker. The reasonableness of this command is obvious. God is a Being of perfect excellence, and the only being of which we have any knowledge, who possesses this character. Goodness or holiness is the only source of real happiness; it is therefore necessary to be holy in order to be happy. As the character of God is the only perfect model of

holiness, it follows that all God's creatures who are intended to be happy, must have the like character. But men will not aim to possess the character of holiness, unless they love it as their chief good. Hence the necessity of loving God with supreme affection.

19. Sin is the source of all evil. If sin was admitted into heaven, it would disturb the happiness of the celestial abode. Hence God has determined that no sinner shall be admitted into heaven. Before men can be received there, they must be purified from sin and sinful propensities. As this world is a state in which men are prepared for heaven, if prepared at all, it is indispensible that while they are in the world, they must be purified in heart, their evil affections must be subdued, and their prevailing dispositions must be holy. Thus when they are sanctified, and supreme love to God prevails in their heart, they become qualified for the enjoyment of bliss with God and other holy beings.

20. It is true, that in this world, men do not become perfectly holy; but God has provided a Redeemer whose example on earth was a perfect model of holy obedience to God's law, which example men are to imitate as far as they are able; and God accepts the penitent sinner's cordial faith in Christ, accompanied with sincere repentance, and humble submission and obedience to his commands, in the place of perfect holiness of character.

21. The duties which you owe directly to God are entire, unwavering faith in his promises, reverence of his character, and frequent prayer and worship. Unbelief is a great sin, and

so is profaneness, irreverence, contempt of his character and laws, neglect of prayer and of worship, public and private. All worship of images, and saints is an abomination to God; it is idolatry which is strictly forbidden in the Bible; and all undue attachment to pleasures, the amusements, and honors of the world, is a species of idolatry.

22. The second class of duties comprehends all such as you are bound to perform to your fellow men. These duties are very numerous, and require to be studied with care. The general law on this subject, is prescribed by Christ in these words, "Thou shalt love thy neighbor as thyself." You are bound to do that to others which you desire them to do to you. This law includes all the duties of respect to superiors, and of justice and kindness to all men.

23. It has already been stated to you, that you are to obey your parents; and although obedience to other superiors may not always be required of you, yet you are bound to yield them due honor and respect in all the concerns of life. Nothing can be more improper than a neglect or violation of this respect. It is a beautiful anecdote, recorded of the Spartan youth, that in a public meeting, young persons rose from their seats, when a venerable old man entered the assembly. It makes no difference whether the aged man is an acquaintance or a stranger; whoever he may be, always give him the precedence. In public places, and at public tables, it is extreme rudeness and ill manners, for the young to thrust themselves into the highest and best seats.

24. The law of kindness extends also to the treatment of equals. Civility requires that to them all persons should give a preference; and if they do not accept it, the offer always manifests good breeding, and wins affection. Never claim too much; modesty will usually gain more than is demanded; but arrogance will gain less. Modest, unassuming manners conciliate esteem; bold, obtrusive manners excite resentment or disgust.

25. As mankind are all one family, the rule of loving our neighbor as ourselves, extends to the performance of all duties of kindness to persons of all nations and all conditions of men. Persons of all nations, of all ranks, and conditions, high and low, rich and poor, and all sects or denominations, are our brethren, and our *neighbors* in the sense that Christ intended to use the word in his precept. This comprehensive rule of duty cannot be limited by any acts of our own. Any private association of men for the practice of contracting the rule, and confining our benevolence[4] to such associations, is a violation of the divine commands. Christ healed the sick, and the lame, without any regard to the nation or sect to which they belonged.

26. One of the most important rules of social conduct is *justice*. This consists positively in rendering to every person what is due to him and negatively, in avoiding everything that may impair his rights Justice embraces the rights of property, the rights of personal liberty and safety, and the rights of character.

---

[4] An inclination to perform kind, charitable acts -

27. In regard to property, you are to pay punctually all your just debts. When a debt becomes payable to another, you cannot withhold or delay payment without a violation of his right. By failure or delay of payment, you keep that which belongs to another. But the rule of justice extends to every act which can affect the property of another. If you borrow any article of your neighbor, you are to use it with care and not injure the value of it. If you borrow a book or any utensil, and injure it, you take a portion of your neighbor's property. Yet heedless people who would not steal twenty five cents from another, often think nothing of injuring a borrowed utensil, to twice or five times that amount.

28. In like manner, one who takes a lease of a house or land, is bound to use it in such a manner as to injure it as little as possible. Yet how often do the lessees of real estate, strive to gain as much as possible from the use of it, while they suffer the buildings and fences to go to ruin, to the great injury of the owner! This is one of the most common species of immorality. But all needless waste and all diminution of the value of the property in the hands of a lessee, proceeding from negligence, amounts to the same thing as the taking of so much of the owner's property without the right. It is not considered as stealing, but it is a species of fraud that is as really immoral as stealing.

29. The command of God, "Thou shalt not steal," is very comprehensive, extending to the prohibition of every species of fraud. Stealing is the taking of something from the possession of another clandestinely for one's own use. This may be done

by entering the house of another at night, and taking his property; or by taking goods from a shop secretly or by entering upon another's land and taking his horse or his sheep. These customary modes of stealing are punishable by law.

30. But, there are many other ways of taking other men's property secretly, which are not so liable to be detected. If a stone is put into a bag of cotton intended for a distant market, it increases the weight, and the purchaser of the bag who pays for it at its weight, buys a stone instead of it weight in cotton. In this case, the man who first sells the bag knowing it contains a stone, takes from the purchaser by fraud as much money as the weight of the stone produces, that is, as much as the same weight of cotton is worth. This is as criminal as it would be to enter his house and steal so much money.

31. If butter or lard is put up for foreign or distant market, it should be put up in a good state, and the real quality should be as it *appears* to be. If any deception is practiced, by covering that which is bad by that which is good or by any other means, all the price of the article which it brings beyond the real worth, is so much money taken from the purchaser by fraud, which falls within the criminality of stealing. If a buyer of the article in Europe or the West Indies is thus defrauded, *he* may never be able to know who has done the wrong; but God knows and will punish the wrong doer. It is immoral to cheat a foreigner as to cheat a neighbor.

32. Not only property in money and goods is to be respected; but the property in fruit growing in orchards and gardens. A man's apples, pears, peaches, and melons are as

entirely his own, as his goods or coin. Every person who climbs over a fence or enters by a gate into another's enclosure without permission is a trespasser; and if he takes fruit secretly, he is a thief. It makes no difference that a pear or an apple or a melon is of small value; a man has as exclusive a right to a *cent* or a *melon* as he does to a *dollar*, a *dime* or an *eagle*.[5]

33. If in a country where apples are abundant, men do not notice the taking of a few apples to eat, yet this indulgence is not to be considered as giving a right to take them. Where the injury is trifling, men in neighborhoods may do such things by consent. But there are many species of fruit so rare as to be cultivated with so much labor and protected with care. Such fruit is often valued even more than money. The stealing of such fruit is one of the most common crimes, and as disgraceful to a civilized and Christian people as it is common. Let every man or boy who enters another's enclosure and steals his fruit be assured he is guilty as one who enters another's house and takes the same value in money.

34. If in making payment or counting money, a mistake occurs by which a sum falls into your hands, which belongs to another person, you are as much bound by moral duty to correct the mistake and restore the money to the rightful owner, as you would *be* not to take it by theft. If persons suppose that because this money falls into their hands by mistake, and the mistake may never be known to the person

---

[5] A gold coin once used in the United States, stamped with an eagle on the reverse side and having a face value of ten dollars.

who has the right to the money; this makes no difference in the point of morality; the concealment of the mistake and the keeping of the money are dishonest, and fall within the command "Thou shalt not steal."

35. When a man is hired to work for another by the day, the week or the month, he is bound to perform what he undertakes; and if no particular amount of labor is promised, he is bound to do the work that is ordinarily done in such cases. If a man hired to do a day's work spends half the day in idleness, he defrauds his employer of a part of his due; that is of one half the value of the day's labor. If the price of labor is one dollar for the day, then to waste half the day in idleness is to defraud the employer of half a dollar from his chest.

36. When a mechanic contracts to build a house or a ship, he is bound to perform the work in the manner which is promised. If he performs the work slightly, and with workmanship inferior to that which is promised and understood at the time of contracting, he defrauds his employer. Neglect of duty, in such a case, is as essentially immoral as the positive act of taking property from another without his consent.

37. The adulteration[6] of liquors and drugs is extremely criminal. By adulteration, the value of a thing is diminished; and if an adulterated liquor or drug is sold for that which is genuine, a fraud is committed on the purchaser. The adulteration of wines is one of the most common and flagrant

---

[6] To make impure by adding extraneous, improper, or inferior ingredients -

immoralities in commercial countries. The adulteration of drugs may be even more iniquitous, for then the physician cannot rely on their effects in healing the sick. All classes of people, but especially the common people, are continually subjected to frauds by such adulterations. A glass of genuine unadulterated wine is scarcely found, and foul mixtures are often used as medicines, for no pure wine is to be had in the neighborhood.

38. The modes used to defraud men in the kind or in the quantity or quality of commodities offered for sale, are almost innumerable. They extend to almost everything in which fraud is not easily detected. This is a melancholy picture of the state of society; exhibiting unequivocal evidence of the depravity of men. It shows that the love of money is the root of all evil - a principle so powerful in the human heart as to overcome all regard to truth, morality and reputation.

39. In all your dealings with men, let a strict regard to veracity and justice govern all your actions. Uprightness in dealings secures confidence and the confidence of our fellow men is the basis of reputation, and often a source of prosperity. Men are always ready to assist those whom they can trust; and a good character in men of business often raises them to wealth and distinction. On the other hand hypocrisy, trickishness, and want of punctuality and of fairness in trade often sink men into meanness and poverty. Hence we see that the divine commands, which require men to be just, are adapted to advance their temporal as well as spiritual interest.

40. Not only are theft and fraud of all kinds forbidden by the laws of God and man, but all kinds of injury or annoyance of the peace, security, rights and prosperity of men. The practice of boys and of men, who do mischief for sport, is as wrong in morality as it is degrading to the character. To pull down or deface a sign-board; to break or deface a mile-stone; to cut and disfigure benches or tables, in a school house, court house or church; to place obstacles in the highway; to pull down or injure fences; to tarnish the walls of houses or the boards of a fence, and similar tricks that injure property or disturb the peace of society, are not only mean but immoral. Why will rational beings indulge in such feats of mischief and folly? Men are not made to injure and annoy one another; but to assist them; not to do harm, but to do good; not to lessen but to increase the prosperity and enjoyments of their fellow men.

41. But you are required to be just not only to the property, but to the reputation of others. A man's reputation is dearer to him than his property, and he that detracts from the good name of another is as criminal as the thief who takes his property. Say nothing of your neighbor maliciously, nor spread reports about him to lessen his reputation. On the other hand vindicate his conduct in all cases when you can do it with a clear conscience. If you cannot defend it, remain silent.

42. Nor are you to be less careful of the rights of others, than of their reputation, and property. By the laws of creation, and by our civil constitution, all men have equal rights to protection, to liberty, and to free enjoyment of all the benefits

and privileges of government. All secret attempts, by associations or otherwise to give one set of men or one party, advantages over another, are mean, dishonorable and immoral. All secret combinations of men to gain for themselves or their party, advantages in preferments[7] to office, are trespasses upon the rights of others.

43. In every condition of life, and in forming your opinions on every subject, let it be an established principle in regulating your conduct, that nothing can be *honorable* which is *morally wrong*. Men who disregard or disbelieve revelation often err from the true standard of honor, by substituting public opinion or false maxims for the divine laws. The character of God, his holy attributes, and perfect law constitute the only models and rules of excellence and true honor. Whatever deviates from these models and rules must be wrong, and dishonorable. Crime and vice are therefore not only repugnant to duty, and to human happiness; but are always derogatory to reputation. All vice implies defect and meaning in human character.

44. In whatever laudable occupation you are destined to labor, be steady in an industrious application of time. Time is given to you for employment, not for waste. Most men are obliged to labor for subsistence; and this is a happy arrangement of things by divine appointment; as labor is one of the best preservatives both of health and of moral habits. But if you are not under the necessity of laboring for subsistence, let your time be occupied in something which shall

---

[7] The act of advancing to a higher position or office; promotion -

do good to yourselves and your fellow men. Idleness tends to lend men into vicious pleasures: and to waste time is to abuse the gifts of God.

45. With most persons, the gaining of property is a primary object, and one which demands wisdom in planning business, and assiduous care, attention and industry in conducting it. But it is perhaps more difficult to keep property than to gain it; as men while acquiring property are more economical and make more careful calculations of profit and loss, than when they hold large possessions. Men who inherit large possessions are particularly liable to waste their property, and fall into poverty. The greatest hereditary estates in this country are usually dissipated by the second or third generation. The sons and grandsons of the richest men are often hewers of wood and drawers of water to the sons and grandsons of their father's and grandfather's servants.

46. As a general rule in the expenditure of money, it is safest to earn money before you spend it, and to spend every year less than you earn. By this means, you will secure a comfortable subsistence, and be enabled to establish your children in some honest calling; at the same time, this practice will furnish the means of contributing to the wants of the poor, and to the promotion of institutions for civilizing and christianizing heathen nations. This is a great and indispensable duty.

47. In your mode of living, be not ambitious of adopting every extravagant fashion. Many fashions are not only inconvenient and expensive, but inconsistent with good taste.

The love of finery is of savage origin; the rude inhabitant of the forest delights to deck his person with pieces of shining metal, with painted feathers, and with some appendage dangling from the ears or nose. The same love of finery infects civilized men and women, more or less in every country, and the body is adorned with brilliant gems and gaudy attire. But true taste demands great simplicity of dress. A well made person is one of the most beautiful of all God's works, and a simple, neat dress displays this person to the best advantage.

48. In all sensual indulgences be temperate. God has given to men all good things for use and enjoyments; but enjoyment consists in using food and drink only for nourishment and sustenance of the body, and all amusements and indulgences should be in moderation. Excess never affords enjoyment; but always brings inconvenience, pain or disease. In selecting food and drink, take such as best support the healthy functions of the body, avoid as much as possible, the stimulus of high-seasoned food; and reject the use of ardent spirits, as the most fatal poison.

49. When you become entitled to exercise the right of voting for public officers, let it be impressed on your mind that God commands you to choose for rulers, *just men who will rule in the fear of God*. The preservation of a republican government depends on the faithful discharge of this duty; if the citizens neglect their duty and place unprincipled men in office, the government will soon be corrupted; laws will be made, not for the public good, so much as for selfish or local purposes; corrupt or incompetent men will be appointed to execute laws;

the public revenues will be squandered on unworthy men; and the rights of the citizens will be violated or disregarded. If a republican government fails to secure public prosperity and happiness, it must be because the citizens neglect the divine commands, and elect bad men to make and administer the laws. Intriguing men can never be safely trusted.

50. To young men I would recommend that their treatment of females should be always characterized by kindness, delicacy and respect. The tender sex look to men for protection and support. Females when properly educated and devoted to their appropriate duties, are qualified to add greatly to the happiness of society, and of domestic life. Endowed with finer sensibilities than men, they are quick to learn and to practice the civilities and courtesies of life; their reputation requires the nice observance of the rules of decorum; and their presence and example impose most salutary restraints on the ruder passions and less polished manners of the other sex.

In the circle of domestic duties, they are cheerful companions of their husbands; they give grace and joy to prosperity; consolation and support to adversity. When we see an affectionate wife devoted to her domestic duties, cheering her husband with smiles, and as a mother, carefully tending and anxiously guarding her children and forming their minds to virtue and to piety; or watching with conjugal or maternal tenderness over the bed of sickness: we cannot fail to number among the chief temporal advantages of Christianity, the elevation of the female character. Let justice then be done to their merits; guard their purity; defend their honor; treat them with tenderness and respect.

51. For a knowledge of the human heart, and the characters of men, it is customary to resort to the writings of Shakespeare, and of other dramatic authors, and to biography, novels, tales and fictitious narratives. But whatever amusement may be derived from such writngs, they are not the best authorities for a knowledge of mankind. The most perfect maxims and examples for regulating your social conduct and domestic economy, as well as the best rules of morality and religion, are to be found in the Bible. The history of the Jews presents the true character of man in all its forms. All the traits of human characters, good and bad; all the passions of the human heart; all the principles which guide and misguide men in society, and depicted in that short history, with an artless simplicity that has no parallel in modern writings. As to maxims of wisdom or prudence, the Proverbs of Solomon furnish a complete system, and sufficient, if carefully observed, to make any man wise, prosperous and happy. The observation, that "a soft answer turneth away wrath," if strictly observed by men, would prevent half the broils and contentions that inflict wretchedness on society and families.

52. Let your first care, through life, be directed to support and extend the influence of the Christian religion, and the observance of the Sabbath. This is the only system of religion which has ever been offered to the consideration and acceptance of men, which has even probable evidence of a divine original ; It is the only religion that honors the

character and moral government of the Supreme Being : it is the only religion which gives even a probable account of the origins of the world, and of the dispensations of God towards mankind ; it is the only religion which teaches the character and laws of God, with our relations and our duties to him : it is the only religion which assures us of an immortal existence ; which offer means of everlasting salvation, and consoles mankind under the inevitable calamities of the present life.

53. But were we assured that there is to be no future life, and that men are to perish at death like the beasts of the field; the moral principles and precepts contained in the scriptures ought to form the basis of all our civil constitutions and laws. These principles and precepts have truth, immutable truth, for their foundation; and they are adapted to the wants of men in every condition of life. They are the best principles and precepts, because they are exactly adapted to secure the practice of universal justice and kindness among men; and of course to prevent crimes, war and disorders in society. No human laws dictated by different principles from those in the gospel, can ever secure these objects. All the miseries and evils which men suffer from vice, crime, ambition, injustice, oppression, slavery and war, proceed from their despising or neglecting the precepts contained in the Bible.

54. As the means of temporal happiness, then, the Christian religion ought to be received, and maintained with firm and cordial support. It is the real source of all genuine republican principles. It teaches the equality of men as to rights and duties; and while it forbids all oppression, it commands due

subordination to law and rulers. It requires the young to yield obedience to their parents, and enjoins upon men the duty of selecting their rulers from their fellow citizens of mature age, sound wisdom and real religion - "men who fear God and hate covetousness.[8]" The ecclesiastical establishments of Europe which serve to support tyrannical governments, are not the Christian religion, but abuses and corruptions of it. The religion of Christ and his apostles, in its primitive simplicity and purity, unencumbered with the trappings of power and the pomp of ceremonies, is the surest basis of a republican government.

55. Never cease then to give to religion, to its institutions and to its ministers your strenuous support. The clergy in this country are not possessed of rank and wealth; they depend for their influence on their talents and learning, on their private virtues and public services. They are the firm supporters of law and good order, the friends of peace, the expounders and teachers of Christian doctrines, the instructors of youth, the promoters of benevolence, of charity, and of all useful improvements. During the war of the revolution, the clergy were generally friendly to the cause of the country. The present generation can hardly have a tolerable idea of the influence of the New England clergy, in sustaining the patriotic exertions of the people, under appalling discouragements of the war. The writer remembers their good offices with gratitude. Those men therefore who attempt to impair the influence of that respectable order, in this country,

---

[8] Generally, an unreasonable desire for what we do not possess.

attempt to undermine the best supports of religion; and those who destroy the influence and authority of the Christian religion, sap the foundations of public order, of liberty and of republican government.

56. For instruction then in social, religious and civil duties resort to the scriptures for the best precepts and most excellent examples for imitation. The example of unhesitating faith and obedience in Abraham, when he promptly prepared to offer his son Isaac, as a burnt offering, at the command of God, is a perfect model of that trust in God which becomes dependent beings. The history of Joseph furnishes one of the most charming examples of fraternal affection and filial duty and respect of a venerable father, ever exhibited in human life. Christ and his apostles presented, in their lives, the most perfect example of disinterested benevolence, unaffected kindness, humility, patience in adversity, forgiveness of injuries, love to God and all mankind. If men would universally cultivate these religious affections and virtuous dispositions, and with as much diligence as they cultivate human science, and refinement of manners, the world would soon become a terrestrial paradise.

Noah Webster's "Moral Catechism"

Question. What is moral virtue?

Answer. It is an honest upright conduct in all our dealings with men.

Q. Can we always determine what is honest and just?

A. Perhaps not in every instance, but in general it is not difficult.

Q. What rules have we to direct us?

A. God's word contained in the Bible has furnished all necessary rules to direct our conduct.

Q. In what part of the Bible are these rules to be found?

A. In almost every part; but the most important duties between men are summed up in the beginning of Matthew, in Christ's Sermon on the Mount.

Of Humility

Q. What is humility?

A. A lowly temper of mind.

Q. What are the advantages of humility?

A. The advantages of humility in this life are very numerous and great. The humble man has few or no enemies. Everyone loves him and is ready to do him good. If he is rich and prosperous, people do not envy him; if he is poor and unfortunate, every one pities him, and is disposed to alleviate his distresses.

Q. *What is pride?*

A. A lofty high minded disposition.

Q. *Is pride commendable?*

A. By no means. A modest self-approving opinion of our own good deeds is very right. It is natural; it is agreeable; and a spur to good actions. But we should not suffer our hearts to be blown up with pride, whatever great and good deeds we have done; for pride brings upon us the will of mankind, and displeasure of our Maker. ...

Of Mercy

Q. *What is mercy?*

A. It is tenderness of heart.

Q. *What are the advantages of this virtue?*

A. The exercise of it tends to happify every one about us. Rulers of a merciful temper will make their good subjects happy; and will not torment the bad, with needless severity. Parents and masters will not abuse their children and servants with harsh treatment. More love, more confidence, more happiness, will subsist among men, and of course society will be happier.

Of Justice

Q. *What is justice?*

A. It is giving to every man his due.

Q. *Is it always easy to know what is just?*

A. It is generally easy; and where -there is any difficulty in determining, let a man consult the golden rule—"To do to others, what he could reasonably wish they should do to him, in the same circumstances."

Of Truth

Q. *What is truth?*

A. It is speaking and acting agreeable to fact.

Q. *Is it a duty to speak truth at all times?*

A. If we speak at all, we should tell the truth. It is not always necessary to tell what we know. There are many things which concern ourselves and others, which we had better not publish to the world.

Of Charity and Giving Alms[9]

Q. *What is charity?*

A. It signifies giving to the poor, or it is a favorable opinion of men and their actions.

Q. *When and how far is it our duty to give to the poor?*

A. When others really want what we can spare without material injury to ourselves, it is our duty to give them something to relieve their wants.

---

[9] Something (as money or food) given freely to relieve the poor -

Q. When persons are reduced to want by their own laziness and vices, by drunkenness, gambling and the like, is it a duty to relieve them?

A. In general it is not. The man who gives money and provisions to a lazy vicious man, becomes a partaker of his guilt. Perhaps it may be right, to give such a man a meal of victuals to keep him from starving, and it is certainly right to feed his wife and family, and make them comfortable.

Of Avarice

Q. What is avarice?

A. An excessive desire of gaining wealth.

Q. Is this commendable?

A. It is not; but one of the meanest of vices. ...

Of Frugality and Economy

Q. What is the distinction between frugality and avarice?

A. Frugality is a prudent saving of property from needless waste. Avarice gathers more and spends less than is wanted.

Q. What is economy?

A. It is frugality in expenses--it is a prudent management of one's estate. It disposes of property for useful purposes without waste.

Q. How far does true economy extend?

A. To the saving of everything which it is not necessary to spend for comfort and convenience; and the keeping one's expenses within his income or earnings.

Q. What is wastefulness?

A. It is the spending of money for what is not wanted. If a man drinks a dram, which is not necessary for him, or buys a cane which he does not want, he wastes his money. He injures himself, as much as if he had thrown away his money.

Of Industry

Q. What is industry?

A. It is a diligent attention to business in our several occupations.

Q. Is labor a curse or a blessing?

A. Hard labor or drudgery is often a curse by making life toilsome and painful. But constant moderate labor is the greatest blessing.

Q. Why then do people complain of it?

A. Because they do not know the evils of not laboring. Labor keeps the body in health, and makes men relish all their enjoyments. "The sleep of the laboring man is sweet," so is his food. He walks cheerfully and whistling about his fields or shop, and scarcely knows pain.

The rich and indolent first lose their health for want of action –
They turn pale, their bodies are enfeebled, they lose their
appetite for food and sleep, they yawn out a tasteless stupid
life without pleasure, and often useless to the world.

Q. What are the other good effects of industry?

A. One effect is to procure an estate. Our Creator has kindly
united our duty, our interest and happiness: for the same labor
which makes us healthy and cheerful, gives us wealth.

Another good effect of industry is, it keeps men from vice. Not
all the moral discourses ever delivered to mankind, have so
much influence in checking the bad passions of men, in keeping
order and peace, and maintaining moral virtue, in society as
industry. Business is a source of health; of prosperity, or virtue,
and obedience to law.

To make good subjects and good citizens, the first requisite is
to educate every young person, in some kind of business. The
possession of millions should not excuse a young man from
application to business, and that parent or guardian who
suffers his child or his ward to be bred in indolence, becomes
accessory to the vices and disorders of society, he is guilty of
"not providing for his household, and is worse than an infidel."

Of Cheerfulness

Q. Is cheerfulness a virtue?

A. It doubtless is, and a moral duty to practice it.

Q. Can we be cheerful when we please?

A. In general it depends much on ourselves. We can often
mould our temper into a cheerful frame --We can frequent
company and other objects calculated to inspire us with

cheerfulness. To indulge a habitual gloominess of mind is weakness and sin.

Q. What are the effects of cheerfulness on ourselves?

A. Cheerfulness is a great preservative of health, over which it is our duty to watch with care. We have no right to sacrifice our health by the indulgence of a gloomy state of mind. Besides, a cheerful man will do more business and do it better than a melancholy one.

Q. What are the effects of cheerfulness on others?

A. Cheerfulness is readily communicated to others, by which means their happiness is increased. We are all influenced by sympathy, and naturally partake of the joys and sorrows of others.

Q. What effect has melancholy on the heart?

A. It hardens and benumbs it. It chills the warm affections of love and friendship, and prevents the exercise of the social passions. A melancholy person's life is all night and winter. It is as unnatural as perpetual darkness and frost.

Q. What shall one do when overwhelmed with grief?

A. The best method of expelling grief from the mind, or of quieting its pains, is to change the objects that are about us; to ride from place to place and frequent cheerful company. It is our duty so to do, especially when grief sits heavy on the heart.

Q. Is it not right to grieve for the loss of near friends?

A. It is certainly right, but we should endeavor to moderate our grief, and not suffer it to impair our health, or to grow into a settled melancholy. The use of grief is to soften the heart and make us better. But when our friends are dead, we can render them no further service. Our duty to them ends, when we commit them to the grave; but our duty to ourselves, our families and surviving friends, requires that we perform to them the customary offices of life. We should therefore remember our departed friends only to imitate their virtue; and not to pine away with useless sorrow.

Q. Has not religion a tendency to fill the mind with gloom?

A. True religion never has this effect. Superstition and false notions of God often make men gloomy; but true rational piety and religion have the contrary effect. They fill the man with joy and cheerfulness; and the countenance of a truly pious man should always wear a secure simile.

Q. What has Christ said concerning gloomy Christians?

A. He has pronounced them hypocrites; and commanded his followers not to copy their sad countenances and disfigured faces; but even in their acts of humiliation to "anoint their hands and wash their feet." Christ intended by this, that religion does not consist in, nor require a monkish sadness and gravity; on the other hand he intimates that such appearance of sanctity is generally the marks of hypocrisy. He expressly enjoins upon his followers, marks of cheerfulness. Indeed the only true ground of perpetual cheerfulness, is a consciousness of ever having done well, and an assurance of divine favor.

Noah Webster's "Federal Catechism"

A short EXPLANATION *of the* CONSTITUTION *of the*
UNITED STATES OF AMERICA, *and the* PRINCIPLES *of*
GOVERNMENT
For the Use of Schools

Q. *What is a constitution of government?*

A. A constitution of government, or a political constitution,
consists in certain standing rules or ordinances, agreed upon by
a nation or state, determining the manner in which the
supreme power shall be exercised over that nation or state, or
rather how the legislative body shall be formed.

Q. *How many kinds of constitutions are there; or in how many
ways may the sovereign power be exercised over a people?*

A. Constitutions are commonly divided into three kinds;
monarchy, aristocracy, and democracy.

Q. *Explain the sorts of government.*

A. When the sovereign power is exercised by one person, the
constitution is a monarchy. When a few rich men, or nobles,
have the whole supreme power in their hands, the constitution
is an aristocracy. When the supreme power is exercised by all
the citizens, in a general meeting or assembly, the constitution
is a democracy.

Q. *What are the faults of despotic governments?*

A. In a despotic government, a whole nation is at the disposal of one person. If this person, the prince, is of a cruel or tyrannical disposition, he may abuse his subjects, take away their lives, their property, or their liberty.

Q. *What objections are there to aristocracy?*

A. In an aristocracy, where a few rich men govern, the poor may be oppressed, the nobles may make laws to suit themselves and ruin the common people. Besides, the nobles, having equal power one with another, may quarrel and throw the state into confusion; in this case there is no person of superior power to settle the dispute.

Q. *What are the defects of democracy?*

A. In democracy, where the people all meet for the purpose of making laws, there are commonly tumults and disorders. A small city may sometimes be governed in this manner; but if the citizens are numerous, their assemblies make a crowd or mob, where debates cannot be carried on with coolness and candor, nor can arguments be heard: Therefore a pure democracy is generally a very bad government. It is often the most tyrannical government on earth; for a multitude is often rash, and will not hear reason.

Q. *Is there another and better form of government than any of these?*

A. There is. A representative republic, in which the people freely choose deputies to make laws for them, is much the best form of government hitherto invented.

Q. What are the peculiar advantages of representative governments?

A. When deputies or representatives are chosen to make laws, they will commonly consult the interest of the people who choose them, and if they do not, the people can choose others in their room. Besides, the deputies coming from all parts of a state, bring together all the knowledge and information necessary to show the true interest of the whole state; at the same time, being but few in number, they can hear arguments and debate peaceably on a subject. But the great security of such a government is, that the men who make laws, are to be governed by them; so that they are not apt to do wrong willfully. When men make laws for themselves, as well as for their neighbors, they are led by their own interest to make good laws.

Q. Which of the forms or kinds of government is adopted by the American States?

A. The states are all governed by constitutions that fall under the name of representative republics. The people choose deputies to act for them in making laws; and in general, the deputies, when assembled, have as full power to make and repeal laws, as the whole body of freemen would have, if they were collected for the same purpose.

Q. By what name may we call the United States in their political capacity?

A. A federal representative republic.

Q. How are the powers of government divided?

A. Into the legislative, judicial, and executive.

Q. *What is meant by a legislative power?*

A. By legislative is understood that body or assembly of men who have the power of making laws and regulations for governing the state.

Q. *Where does the power of making laws for the United States reside?*

A. By the constitution of the United States, the power of making laws is given to the representatives of the people chosen by the people or their legislatures, and assembled in two distinct houses. This body of representatives so assembled, is called "the Congress of the United States."

Q. *What are the two separate houses called?*

A. One is called the Senate, the other is the house of Representatives.

Q. *How is the senate formed.*

A. By two delegates from each state, chosen by the legislature of the state, for six years.

Q. *Why are not senators chosen every year?*

A. Because one branch of Congress is designed to be distinguished for firmness and knowledge of business.

Q. *How is the house of representatives formed?*

A. This branch of the national legislature is composed of delegates from the several states, chosen by the people, every second year.

Q. *Can every man in the states vote for delegates to Congress?*

A. By no means. In almost every state some property is necessary to give a man a right to vote. In general, men who have no estate, pay no taxes, and who have no settled habitation, are not permitted to vote for rulers, because they have no interest to secure, they may be vagabonds or dishonest men, and may be bribed by the rich.

Q. *Why is congress divided into two houses?*

A. When the power of making laws is vested in a single assembly, bills may often pass without due deliberation. Whole assemblies of men may be rash, hasty, passionate, tumultuous, and whenever this happens it is safe to have some check to their proceedings, that they may not inure the public. One house therefore may be a check upon the other.

Q. *Why may Congress regulate the election of its own members or why is not this power left entirely to the states?*

A. For this good reason; a few states might by neglect, delay or willfulness, prevent the meeting of a Congress, and destroy the federal government. It is necessary that Congress should have power to oblige the State to choose delegates, so that they may preserve their own existence.

Q. *It is not unjust that all should be bound to obey a law, when all do not consent to it?*

A. Everything is JUST in government which is NECESSARY to the PUBLIC GOOD. It is impossible to bring all men to think alike on all subjects, so that if we wait for all opinions to be alike respecting laws, we shall have no laws at all.

Q. *How are the members of Congress paid?*

A. Out of the treasury of the United States, according to a law of Congress.

Q. *Would it not be politic to refuse them a reward, and let them serve their country for the honor of it?*

A. In such a case none but rich men could afford to serve as delegates; the government would then be wholly in the hands of the wealthy; whereas there are many men of little property, who are among the most able, wise and honest persons in a state.

Q. *How far do the powers of Congress extend?*

A. The powers of Congress extend to the regulation of all matters of a GENERAL NATURE, or such as concern ALL the United States.

Q. *Will not this national government in time destroy the state governments?*

A. It is not probable this will be the case; indeed the national government is the best security of the state governments; for each state has pledged itself to support every state government. If it were not for our union a powerful state might conquer its weaker neighbor, and with this addition of power, conquer the next state, and so on, till the whole would be subject to one ambitious state.

FINIS

No truth is more evident to my mind than that the Christian religion must be the basis of any government intended to secure the rights and privileges of a free people.